FOUR GREAT LOVES

JUDITH ALLEN SHELLY

8 STUDIES
FOR INDIVIDUALS
OR GROUPS

CW00953632

Life
Builder
Study

INTER-VARSITY PRESS
36 Causton Street, London SW1P 4ST, England
Email: ivp@ivpbooks.com
Website: www.ivpbooks.com

© Judith Allen Shelly, 2003, 2012, 2018

Judith Allen Shelly has asserted her right under the Copyright, Designs and Patents Act 1988 to be identified as Author of this work.

All rights reserved. No part of this publication may be reproduced, stored in a retrieval system, or transmitted, in any form or by any means, electronic, mechanical, photocopying, recording or otherwise, without the prior permission of the publisher or the Copyright Licensing Agency.

Scripture quotations are taken from The Holy Bible, New International Version. Copyright © 1973, 1978, 1984 by International Bible Society. Anglicization copyright © 1979, 1984, 1989. Used by permission of Hodder & Stoughton Publishers, a member of the Hachette UK Group. All rights reserved. 'NIV' is a registered trademark of International Bible Society. UK trademark number 1448790.

Originally published in the United States of America in the LifeGuide® Bible Studies series in 2003 by InterVarsity Press, Downers Grove, Illinois
First published in Great Britain by Scripture Union in 2012
This edition published in Great Britain by Inter-Varsity Press 2018

British Library Cataloguing-in-Publication Data
A catalogue record for this book is available from the British Library.

ISBN: 978–1–78359–817–5

Printed in Great Britain by Ashford Colour Press Ltd, Gosport, Hampshire

Inter-Varsity Press publishes Christian books that are true to the Bible and that communicate the gospel, develop discipleship and strengthen the church for its mission in the world.

IVP originated within the Inter-Varsity Fellowship, now the Universities and Colleges Christian Fellowship, a student movement connecting Christian Unions in universities and colleges throughout Great Britain, and a member movement of the International Fellowship of Evangelical Students. Website: www.uccf.org.uk. That historic association is maintained, and all senior IVP staff and committee members subscribe to the UCCF Basis of Faith.

Contents

Getting the Most Out of
Four Great Loves

Love makes the world go 'round. At least that's how the old song goes. But we live in a broken, love-starved world. Relationships go sour. Families squabble and sometimes hurt us. Friends disappoint us. Even the church can add to our sense of aloneness.

The Bible gives us hope and encouragement. It reveals that we are called to be a loving community—loving God, loving God's Word, loving God's people in all their diversity and loving God's purposes in the world. That's an awesome task, but God promises to equip us for it. We can love because God first loved us unconditionally, in spite of our unfaithfulness.

But what does it mean to love God? How can we learn to love God's Word? Who are the people we are called to love? Just what are God's purposes in the world? This set of eight studies examines these questions in the light of Scripture—God's written Word. You'll be amazed at how the Bible provides startling, practical direction for your life today.

Begin each study with prayer and close each session with a time of prayer and worship, expressing your love for God. If you study with others, plan to spend enough time together that you can enjoy one another's fellowship.

Most of all, enjoy discovering new things from God's Word!

Suggestions for Individual Study

1. As you begin each study, pray that God will speak to you through his Word.

2. Read the introduction to the study and respond to the personal reflection question or exercise. This is designed to help you focus on God and on the theme of the study.

3. Each study deals with a particular passage—so that you can delve into the author's meaning in that context. Read and reread the passage to be studied. The questions are written using the language of the New International Version, so you may wish to use that version of the Bible. The New Revised Standard Version is also recommended.

4. This is an inductive Bible study, designed to help you discover for yourself what Scripture is saying. The study includes three types of questions. *Observation* questions ask about the basic facts: who, what, when, where and how. *Interpretation* questions delve into the meaning of the passage. *Application* questions help you discover the implications of the text for growing in Christ. These three keys unlock the treasures of Scripture.

Write your answers to the questions in the spaces provided or in a personal journal. Writing can bring clarity and deeper understanding of yourself and of God's Word.

5. It might be good to have a Bible dictionary handy. Use it to look up any unfamiliar words, names or places.

6. Use the prayer suggestion to guide you in thanking God for what you have learned and to pray about the applications that have come to mind.

7. You may want to go on to the suggestion under "Now or Later," or you may want to use that idea for your next study.

Suggestions for Members of a Group Study

1. Come to the study prepared. Follow the suggestions for individual study mentioned above. You will find that careful preparation will greatly enrich your time spent in group discussion.

2. Be willing to participate in the discussion. The leader of your group will not be lecturing. Instead, he or she will be encouraging the members of the group to discuss what they have learned. The leader will be asking the questions that are found in this guide.

3. Stick to the topic being discussed. Your answers should be based on the verses which are the focus of the discussion and not on outside authorities such as commentaries or speakers. These studies focus on a particular passage of Scripture. Only rarely should you refer to other portions of the Bible. This allows for everyone to participate in in-depth study on equal ground.

4. Be sensitive to the other members of the group. Listen attentively when they describe what they have learned. You may be surprised by their insights! Each question assumes a variety of answers. Many questions do not have "right" answers, particularly questions that aim at meaning or application. Instead the questions push us to explore the passage more thoroughly.

When possible, link what you say to the comments of others. Also, be affirming whenever you can. This will encourage some of the more hesitant members of the group to participate.

5. Be careful not to dominate the discussion. We are sometimes so eager to express our thoughts that we leave too little opportunity for others to respond. By all means participate! But allow others to also.

6. Expect God to teach you through the passage being discussed and through the other members of the group. Pray that you will have an enjoyable and profitable time together, but also that as a result of the study you will find ways that you can take action individually and/or as a group.

7. Remember that anything said in the group is considered confidential and should not be discussed outside the group unless specific permission is given to do so.

8. If you are the group leader, you will find additional suggestions at the back of the guide.

1

Loving God
Through Worship

Psalm 116

This seems to be the age of "worship wars." Christian groups fight over styles of music, liturgical forms, length of the prayers and sermon, whether or not to raise our hands, wave flags, dance, or allow certain gifts of the Spirit to flow. But the psalmist knew that worship was not about personal preferences. For him, worship focused on God. It was a spontaneous overflowing of his love for God.

GROUP DISCUSSION. What aspects of worship most help you to focus on God?

PERSONAL REFLECTION. Think about someone you love deeply. What characteristics of that person do you particularly enjoy?

If you ever felt like being a Christian meant putting on a happy face and faking it when doubts clouded your thoughts, the

Psalms will give you hope. Far from presenting an unrealistic, simplistic view of faith, they show God's faithful people struggling with what it means to love God in the face of fear, discouragement and pain. *Read Psalm 116.*

---

1. Why does the psalmist love God (vv. 1-2, 5-8)?

---

2. Think back to when you first loved God. What drew you to him?

---

3. How does the psalmist respond to God's love (vv. 2, 5, 7, 9, 12-14, 16-19)?

---

4. In what ways can prayer and worship be a barometer for our relationship with God (vv. 1-4, 10-11)?

---

5. Looking through the passage, what different kinds of prayer do you see the psalmist using?

Which of these practices might be helpful to you in your own prayer life?

---

6. Recent research has demonstrated that regular worship attendance is "good for your health." True health is more than the absence of disease. It involves being able to function well in community—physically, emotionally, socially and spiritually. What evidence for this does the psalmist describe (vv. 7-10)?

---

7. How does love for God find expression in worship (vv. 2, 9, 12-14, 17-19)?

---

8. How is your worship an expression of your love for God?

---

9. What things would you like to change about your worship?

Spend a few minutes responding to God in love. Praise him for his attributes, thank him for what he has done, confess your sin and bring your needs and concerns before him.

Now or Later

Read Deuteronomy 6:4-9. What does it mean to love God with all your heart, soul and strength?

According to verses 7-9, how do we develop that love for God?

Why are such constant reminders necessary?

What are some practical ways you could follow these instructions at home and within your community?

2

Loving God
by Serving Others

It was finals week, and I found myself bored with studying but sick with worry over whether I'd do okay on my exams. A friend from my dorm Bible study group stopped by to talk. She'd just broken up with her boyfriend. As we commiserated with one another, she suddenly asked, "What difference does being a Christian make, anyhow? It seems like my life is just as messed up as it always was!"

GROUP DISCUSSION. What difference does being a Christian make in your life?

PERSONAL REFLECTION. Thank God for what his presence has meant in your life just in the last few days.

A former fisherman, Peter had a turbulent relationship with Jesus. One of the first disciples chosen, Peter became part of the inner circle of those who followed Jesus. His love for Jesus enabled him to walk on water (Matthew 14:29), then sink miserably when he doubted. He felt free to rebuke Jesus for predicting his own death, only to be told, "Get behind me, Satan!" (Matthew 16:23). He constantly declared his absolute allegiance to Jesus, then denied him three times when association with Jesus became risky (John 18:15-27). The account in John 21 occurred soon after Jesus rose from the dead. It was the second time he had appeared to his disciples. *Read John 21:1-19.*

---

1. What might Peter have been thinking when he and the other disciples decided to go fishing?

---

2. How did Peter respond when John recognized Jesus?

What may have accounted for his unusual behavior?

---

3. How did Jesus reassure Peter of his love?

---

4. Examine the interchange between Jesus and Peter in verses 15-17. Why do you think Jesus kept asking Peter the same question?

5. What do you think Peter was feeling? (See especially v. 17.)

6. What did Jesus mean by telling Peter to feed and tend his sheep?

7. How does serving others demonstrate our love for Jesus?

8. According to verses 18-19, what consequences would Peter face for his obedience to Jesus?

9. Why do you think Peter followed Jesus anyhow?

10. How do you think Jesus is calling you to serve him?

Who are the "sheep" he is calling you to feed and tend?

---

11. How can you begin doing that, or preparing for it, right now?

Pray, asking God how he wants you to serve others in Jesus' name.

Now or Later

In Matthew 25:31-46 Jesus describes specific ways that he expects us to love him by serving others. Read the passage.

Who are the hungry, thirsty, strangers, naked, sick and imprisoned in your life?

How could you, either as an individual or with a group, serve these people in concrete ways?

3

Loving God's Word
Our Guide for Life

Psalm 119:97-112

One of the most exciting Bible study groups I ever joined was made up primarily of Roman Catholics. It was soon after the Second Vatican Council, an official gathering called by Pope John XXIII, which made sweeping reforms in the Catholic Church, including strongly encouraging laypeople to read the Scriptures. For most in the group, it was as if they were examining a once-forbidden book. They marveled at every word, sought to apply every detail to their lives and eventually formed a lay community to serve the poor. My own casual attitude toward the Bible paled in comparison.

GROUP DISCUSSION. What difference has the Bible made in your life?

PERSONAL REFLECTION. Review your personal history, noting significant milestones and major decisions. To what extent did the Bible affect your choices?

Until the canon (the officially approved text of the Scriptures) was sealed in A.D. 367, the Bible was a work in progress. For the psalmist, it consisted of the Law—the first five books of our Bible. *Read Psalm 119:97-112.*

---

1. Describe the psalmist's attitude toward God's law.

Which of these do you most identify with and why?

---

2. According to this passage, what are the benefits of studying God's Word?

---

3. In what ways can knowledge of Scripture give you more understanding than your teachers (v. 99)?

---

4. How would you respond if you found yourself in a class where the instructor was teaching things that seemed contrary to God's Word? Consider some strategies for respectfully countering the instructor's position.

5. Think about the imagery in verse 105. What difference does a lamp or light make? For example, what might happen if you found yourself lost in the woods after dark without a light?

6. How does the Bible shine on your path in life? Be specific.

7. According to verses 98, 104 and 107-10, how does God's Word prepare us to face enemies?

8. What enemies are you encountering?

How does studying the Bible help you to face them?

9. Describe the ways you are attempting to learn about God's Word at this point in your life.

10. In what ways are the teachings of the Bible a "heritage" for you?

---

11. If you were to make the same commitment as the psalmist in verses 111-12, what would that involve in practical terms?

Close by thanking God specifically for what his Word means to you.

Now or Later

Nehemiah 8:1-18 relates an amazing story about the significance of God's Word for the people of Jerusalem. They had recently been released from captivity by Cyrus, King of Persia. After returning to Jerusalem, they rebuilt the temple and the wall around the city. Although trying to maintain their relationship with God, they had not been exposed to the Scriptures for two generations. To celebrate the completion of the wall they decided to read the Scriptures in the city square. Read the passage, noting how hearing the Scriptures read affected their emotions, thoughts and actions.

4

Loving God's Word
Our Standard for Truth

2 Timothy 3

"Well, I have my truth and you have yours," a friend replies when you express your views about an ethical issue. We live in an age of relativism in which most people believe that we should not make moral judgments because there is no common standard of right and wrong. Theologian and ethicist Stanley Grenz asserts, "We are confronted by the greatest issues humankind has ever faced at a time when the moral fiber of our society appears to be at its weakest."*

GROUP DISCUSSION. What happens in a society where there is no common standard for truth? Give some practical illustrations.

PERSONAL REFLECTION. List all the things that you know are absolutely true.

The Scriptures that Timothy knew were what we call the Old Testament. The New Testament as we know it existed only in the form of widely circulated letters from the apostles and early accounts of Jesus' life and ministry. *Read 2 Timothy 3.*

---

1. How does Paul, the letter's author, describe the culture Timothy will encounter (vv. 1-5)?

How does it compare with your own environment? Give some examples.

---

2. Verses 6-9 describe people who were seeking counterfeit spiritualities. Jannes and Jambres were traditional names of the magicians in Pharaoh's courts who imitated the miracles Moses performed (see Exodus 7:11 and 9:11). What counterfeit spiritualities have you seen (both within the church, the wider community and the media)?

How does Paul describe the effects of counterfeit spiritualities?

3. Contrast the example Paul has set (vv. 10-12) with the "evil men and imposters" described in verse 13.

4. According to verses 14-15, what resources does Timothy have to equip him to face the ungodly environment?

5. Think about the people that most strongly affected your coming to faith and your Christian growth. What were some of the most helpful ways that they did that?

How can you pass on that legacy to others (see 2 Timothy 2:2)?

6. What does Paul say about the Scriptures in verses 16-17?

Why is it important?

7. In what ways can we use the Bible as a teacher—both for ourselves and for others?

8. How have you experienced the Bible correcting and/or equipping you? Give a recent example of when your study of the Scriptures gave you clear direction in a particular situation.

9. In what area or areas of biblical knowledge are you weak?

What step could you take to better know Scripture so that you could be "equipped for every good work"? (Give yourself a small, realistic goal to begin with.)

Praise God for his Word, reflecting specifically on how the Bible has influenced and shaped you.

Now or Later

The Bible records God's absolutes for our lives, including the Ten Commandments (Exodus 20:1-17) and Jesus' great commandments (Matthew 22:37-39). Read through both passages. How are the two related?

Consider each of the Ten Commandments in the light of Jesus' summary of them in Matthew 22. What implications does each commandment have for the activities and decisions facing you this week?

The Moral Quest: Foundations of Christian Ethics (Leicester: Apollos, 1998), p. 17.

5

Loving God's People
in Their Ethnic Diversity

Numbers 12

My children are of Asian descent and sometimes faced prejudice in our mostly Pennsylvania Dutch community. In one particularly upsetting incident, a group of older boys on the school bus pulled their eyes into slits and began chanting at my five-year-old son, "Ching, chang, chop-ted, we know you're adopted!" His seven-year-old sister marched up to them and shouted, "Well, at least we know our parents *wanted* us. I'm not too sure about yours—they *had* to keep you!" Prejudice brings out the worst in all of us.

GROUP DISCUSSION. How welcoming is your community toward people who are different from yourselves (racially, ethnically or socio-economically)?

PERSONAL REFLECTION. List your five closest friends. What racial and ethnic groups do they represent? How have the differences enhanced your friendship? If all of your close friends are from your own ethnic and racial heritage, ask God to show you ways to expand your relationships.

Prior to this passage Moses had been leading the people of Israel through the Sinai Desert for over two years. He had endured a long series of bitter challenges to his leadership, but he also experienced God's affirmation of his leadership and faithful provision for the people, despite their unrealistic demands. His older siblings, Aaron and Miriam, served on his leadership team. Sometime during his travels, Moses had married a Cushite woman. Cush was a country south of Egypt, in the area known as Sudan today. Moses' wife was probably dark-skinned. *Read Numbers 12.*

---

1. Describe how Aaron and Miriam were reacting to their brother's wife.

---

2. How have you, or your friends, used similar arguments (at least in your own mind) against including diverse people in your group activities?

---

3. What else seemed to be at issue besides racial prejudice (v. 2)?

4. In what ways do you see similar mixed agendas in today's racial conflicts?

What do you think people really fear?

---

5. Why do you think verse 3 makes such an issue of Moses' humility?

How could this have been both an asset and a detriment to his leadership?

---

6. How did God deal with Miriam's and Aaron's prejudice and power-mongering?

Why do you think God focused on Moses' character rather than his leadership style?

7. What object lesson did God teach by making Miriam "like snow" with leprosy?

What do you think she experienced during the next seven days of isolation?

8. Think of a situation in which you felt different and out of place. What did you experience, and how did you feel?

9. What attitudes and practices in your fellowship might make new people feel uncomfortable or unwelcome?

10. How could you make people who are different from yourselves feel welcome and accepted?

Spend some time in confession asking God's forgiveness for your own prejudices. Ask God to show you how to become more caring and inclusive toward people who differ from you.

Now or Later

Read Acts 2:1-13. Who was present at Pentecost when the Holy Spirit came upon the crowd?

Find the home countries of those listed in verses 9-11 on a map of the Roman Empire in the first century (you can find one on the Web if you do not have a Bible atlas). What races and cultures may have been represented?

How would you answer the question in verse 12?

6

Loving God's People
into the Kingdom

No one likes being unpopular. We work hard to fit in with our peers—wearing the right clothes, speaking the same language and listening to the same music. We try not to cause conflict. However, sometimes our quest for acceptance causes us to avoid others who don't fit in—the emotionally disturbed, the braggart, the socially inept, the morally questionable or the one who simply talks too much.

GROUP DISCUSSION. Who are the outcasts in your community?

PERSONAL REFLECTION. Recall a time you felt like an outcast. Talk to God about your thoughts and feelings about that time.

The account you will read for this study is a highly unusual encounter. Samaritans were people of mixed race and religion—Jews who had intermarried with foreign invaders. They were scorned by most Jews because they had violated God's warnings against intermarriage and idolatry. Furthermore, women rarely went to the well to draw water at noon. They came at sunset when it was cooler. This was a time to socialize with other village women. In Middle Eastern culture, it was improper for a man to address a woman in public. *Read John 4:4-42.*

---

1. What information does the passage give about this woman's background (see vv. 7-9, 17-18, 20)?

---

2. How do you think the woman feels when Jesus asks her for a drink (vv. 7-12)?

---

3. How does the woman's attitude change as the conversation progresses?

---

4. What do you think created the turning point in the conversation?

5. What attitudes and convictions does the woman express in her arguments?

6. In what ways does Jesus both challenge and affirm her?

7. Note the outcomes of this conversation in verses 27-30. Consider the disciples' response. What do you think they may have been wondering?

How did the woman respond, and what does this tell you about her?

8. Think of someone in your life that you would rather avoid. What bothers you about this person?

What might your friends respond if you started hanging out with this person?

9. How could you show love to this person using some of the same approaches Jesus used?

10. Evangelism often requires a crosscultural exchange, even in our own communities. Who are some of the people God may be calling you to befriend?

Pray for the outcasts in your community, especially those you see on a regular basis. Ask God to show you how to reach out to at least one person that you would rather avoid.

Now or Later

Volunteer, either individually or as a group, to serve at a soup kitchen for the homeless, at a tutoring program, an inner city clinic or summer children's program, or at some other service project to care for those in need.

7

Loving God's Purposes
Trusting God's Plan

Jeremiah 29:1-14

After graduating from college with high honors and great expectations for serving God in her career, my friend Melissa faced a slow job market. Six months later she finally found what appeared to be a good position, but it turned out to be her worst nightmare. Her boss was an alcoholic who manipulated and verbally abused her staff. Her coworkers jealously guarded their own turf, often leaving Melissa feeling inept and alone. She seemed to receive all the assignments that no one else wanted. All her friends advised her to quit, but she couldn't find any good alternatives. She grew angry with God and gradually slipped into a deep sense of hopelessness.

GROUP DISCUSSION. Describe a time when you felt confused about what God wanted you to do with your life.

PERSONAL REFLECTION. As you think about the next five years of your life, what thoughts and feelings come to mind?

Babylon had been attacking Judah for years. The prophet Jeremiah constantly warned the kings of Judah that if they did not return to the Lord, the nation would be taken into exile. However, the more socially accepted prophets were saying that this was merely a short-term problem. The one prophet who agreed with Jeremiah was killed, but Jeremiah continued to prophesy faithfully, saying that Judah might as well surrender to Babylon because God intended to use Babylon to bring Judah to repentance. Eventually, Jeremiah's predictions were realized. *Read Jeremiah 29:1-14.*

---

1. Who are the original recipients of this letter (vv. 1-3)?

---

2. According to verse 4, why are the Israelites in exile?

What difference would it make to know that God had put you in a difficult situation?

In what way can you identify with the Israelites' experience of exile?

3. How does God instruct the Jewish exiles to live during this Babylonian exile in verses 4-9? (Consider the significance of each command to the exiles and to their Babylonian neighbors.)

---

4. Think about a current difficult situation that you hope will be temporary—a job that you dislike, an unpleasant living situation, a class that you would rather not take or a church where you just don't seem to fit in. What difference would it make if you followed the same instructions that God gave to the exiles in Babylon?

How might it affect those around you who do not yet know the Lord?

---

5. What is God's purpose in imposing this seventy-year period of exile, according to verses 10-11?

---

6. What promises does he make to his people in verses 12-14?

7. As you consider your own future, what are your greatest hopes?

How do your hopes compare and contrast to God's plans for his people?

8. What have you learned about yourself, God and others during periods of difficulty?

9. What would it look like in practical terms for you to live according to God's plans in verses 12-14?

10. As Christians, we are to live as "aliens and exiles" (1 Peter 2:11 NSRV) among those who do not know Christ. Think of some practical ways you could do that in your present community, using the principles in this passage so that you might share the hope of Christ with those around you.

Pray specifically for the people you want to share the hope that you have in Christ with. Ask for God's guidance.

Now or Later

Read Genesis 45:4-11. Joseph's brothers had sold him into slavery in a fit of jealousy and revenge. He had lived through slavery and an unjust prison sentence before finally rising to power. At this point in the biblical account, his brothers had come to Egypt seeking relief from famine. They did not know that Joseph was in charge of the storehouses of Egypt. Why do you think Joseph was able to forgive his brothers?

How does knowing that God has a plan for our good give you perspective on the events around you?

8

Loving God's Purposes
A Mission from God

Ephesians 1

"I like being on God's side in this battle," a friend whispered. "We know how it ends!" There's something about having a clear picture of where we're headed that gives us patience with the details and endurance for the long haul. These opening verses of Ephesians give us a broad picture of God's eternal purposes and plan.

GROUP DISCUSSION. How does being a Christian make you any different from those who don't know Christ?

PERSONAL REFLECTION. What do you believe God is calling you to do with your life?

The apostle Paul wrote Ephesians, most likely as a general letter to be circulated among several churches. He was probably in prison at the time. *Read Ephesians 1.*

1. According to verses 3-14, what has God done for us?

Describe a practical difference one of these blessings has made in your life recently.

---

2. What are God's purposes and plans, according to verses 9-10?

How do you see this plan unfolding around you in your community?

in world events?

---

3. What role do you have in fulfilling God's plan to "bring all things together under Christ"?

4. According to verses 11-14, what was involved in your coming to Christ?

5. Examine Paul's prayer in verses 15-23. What does he give thanks for (vv. 15-16)?

6. Who are the people you thank God for, and how have they affected you?

7. Notice Paul's request in verses 17-19. How would your church or fellowship group be different if each person were to experience these things?

8. How have you seen the kind of power from God that is described in verses 19-20 displayed?

9. According to verses 20-23, how is God working to accomplish his purposes in the past, present and future?

---

10. Look at the role God gave the church in verses 22-23. How do you see that mission being fulfilled in your own congregation?

If your church does not have a strong mission focus, how could you help to expand its vision and outreach?

Thank God for the people he has put in your life and the blessings he has given you. Then pray Paul's prayer in verses 17-19. Ask God to show you how he wants you involved in his worldwide mission to unite all things in Christ, and then ask for boldness to follow through. Conclude by praising God for his power and glory.

Now or Later

Read Revelation 21:1-7, 22-27; and 22:1-7. According to these verses, what will life in the New Jerusalem be like?

How will this differ from your present life?

What will this mean in practical terms?

What hope does knowing how the story ends give you in your present situation?

How could you communicate this hope to a friend who does not know Christ?

Leader's Notes

MY GRACE IS SUFFICIENT FOR YOU. (2 COR 12:9)

Leading a Bible discussion can be an enjoyable and rewarding experience. But it can also be *scary*—especially if you've never done it before. If this is your feeling, you're in good company. When God asked Moses to lead the Israelites out of Egypt, he replied, "O LORD, please send someone else to do it" (Ex 4:13). It was the same with Solomon, Jeremiah and Timothy, but God helped these people in spite of their weaknesses, and he will help you as well.

You don't need to be an expert on the Bible or a trained teacher to lead a Bible discussion. The idea behind these inductive studies is that the leader guides group members to discover for themselves what the Bible has to say. This method of learning will allow group members to remember much more of what is said than a lecture would.

These studies are designed to be led easily. As a matter of fact, the flow of questions through the passage from observation to interpretation to application is so natural that you may feel that the studies lead themselves. This study guide is also flexible. You can use it with a variety of groups—student, professional, neighborhood or church groups. Each study takes forty-five to sixty minutes in a group setting.

There are some important facts to know about group dynamics and encouraging discussion. The suggestions listed below should enable you to effectively and enjoyably fulfill your role as leader.

Preparing for the Study

1. Ask God to help you understand and apply the passage in your own life. Unless this happens, you will not be prepared to lead others. Pray too for the various members of the group. Ask God to open your hearts to the message of his Word and motivate you to action.

2. Read the introduction to the entire guide to get an overview of the entire book and the issues which will be explored.

3. As you begin each study, read and reread the assigned Bible passage to familiarize yourself with it.

4. This study guide is based on the New International Version of the Bible. It will help you and the group if you use this translation as the basis for your study and discussion.

5. Carefully work through each question in the study. Spend time in meditation and reflection as you consider how to respond.

6. Write your thoughts and responses in the space provided in the study guide. This will help you to express your understanding of the passage clearly.

7. It might help to have a Bible dictionary handy. Use it to look up any unfamiliar words, names or places. (For additional help on how to study a passage, see chapter five of *How to Lead a LifeBuilder Study*, IVP, 2018.)

8. Consider how you can apply the Scripture to your life. Remember that the group will follow your lead in responding to the studies. They will not go any deeper than you do.

9. Once you have finished your own study of the passage, familiarize yourself with the leader's notes for the study you are leading. These are designed to help you in several ways. First, they tell you the purpose the study guide author had in mind when writing the study. Take time to think through how the study questions work together to accomplish that purpose. Second, the notes provide you with additional background information or suggestions on group dynamics for various questions. This information can be useful when people have difficulty understanding or answering a question. Third, the leader's notes can alert you to potential problems you may encounter during the study.

10. If you wish to remind yourself of anything mentioned in the leader's notes, make a note to yourself below that question in the study.

Leading the Study

1. Begin the study on time. Open with prayer, asking God to help the group to understand and apply the passage.

2. Be sure that everyone in your group has a study guide. Encourage the group to prepare beforehand for each discussion by reading the introduction to the guide and by working through the questions in the study.

3. At the beginning of your first time together, explain that these studies are meant to be discussions, not lectures. Encourage the members of the group to participate. However, do not put pressure on those who may be hesitant to speak during the first few sessions. You may want to suggest the following guidelines to your group.

☐ Stick to the topic being discussed.

☐ Your responses should be based on the verses which are the focus of the discussion and not on outside authorities such as commentaries or speakers.

☐ These studies focus on a particular passage of Scripture. Only rarely should you refer to other portions of the Bible. This allows for everyone to participate in in-depth study on equal ground.

☐ Anything said in the group is considered confidential and will not be discussed outside the group unless specific permission is given to do so.

☐ We will listen attentively to each other and provide time for each person present to talk.

☐ We will pray for each other.

4. Have a group member read the introduction at the beginning of the discussion.

5. Every session begins with a group discussion question. The question or activity is meant to be used before the passage is read. The question introduces the theme of the study and encourages group members to begin to open up. Encourage as many members as possible to participate, and be ready to get the discussion going with your own response.

This section is designed to reveal where our thoughts or feelings need to be transformed by Scripture. That is why it is especially important not to read the passage before the discussion question is asked. The passage will tend to color the honest reactions people would otherwise give because they are, of course, supposed to think the way the Bible does.

You may want to supplement the group discussion question with an icebreaker to help people to get comfortable. See the community section of the *Small Group Starter Kit* (IVP, 1995) for more ideas.

You also might want to use the personal reflection question with your group. Either allow a time of silence for people to respond individually or discuss it together.

6. Have a group member (or members if the passage is long) read aloud the passage to be studied. Then give people several minutes to read the passage again silently so that they can take it all in.

7. Question 1 will generally be an overview question designed to briefly survey the passage. Encourage the group to look at the whole passage, but try to avoid getting sidetracked by questions or issues that will be addressed later in the study.

8. As you ask the questions, keep in mind that they are designed to be used just as they are written. You may simply read them aloud. Or you may prefer to express them in your own words.

There may be times when it is appropriate to deviate from the study guide. For example, a question may have already been answered. If so, move on to the next question. Or someone may raise an important question not covered in the guide. Take time to discuss it, but try to keep the group from going off on tangents.

9. Avoid answering your own questions. If necessary, repeat or rephrase them until they are clearly understood. Or point out something you read in the leader's notes to clarify the context or meaning. An eager group quickly becomes passive and silent if they think the leader will do most of the talking.

10. Don't be afraid of silence. People may need time to think about the question before formulating their answers.

11. Don't be content with just one answer. Ask, "What do the rest of you think?" or "Anything else?" until several people have given answers to the question.

12. Acknowledge all contributions. Try to be affirming whenever possible. Never reject an answer. If it is clearly off-base, ask, "Which verse led you to that conclusion?" or again, "What do the rest of you think?"

13. Don't expect every answer to be addressed to you, even though this will probably happen at first. As group members become more at ease, they will begin to truly interact with each other. This is one sign of healthy discussion.

14. Don't be afraid of controversy. It can be very stimulating. If you don't resolve an issue completely, don't be frustrated. Move on and keep it in mind for later. A subsequent study may solve the problem.

15. Periodically summarize what the group has said about the passage. This helps to draw together the various ideas mentioned and gives continuity to the study. But don't preach.

16. At the end of the Bible discussion you may want to allow group members a time of quiet to work on an idea under "Now or Later." Then discuss what you experienced. Or you may want to encourage group members to work on these ideas between meetings. Give an opportunity during the session for people to talk about what they are learning.

17. Conclude your time together with conversational prayer, adapting the prayer suggestion at the end of the study to your group. Ask for God's help in following through on the commitments you've made.

18. End on time.

Many more suggestions and helps are found in *How to Lead a LifeBuilder Study.*

Components of Small Groups

A healthy small group should do more than study the Bible. There are four components to consider as you structure your time together.

Nurture. Small groups help us to grow in our knowledge and love of God. Bible study is the key to making this happen and is the foundation of your small group.

Community. Small groups are a great place to develop deep friendships with other Christians. Allow time for informal interaction before and after each study. Plan activities and games that will help you get to know each other. Spend time having fun together—going on a picnic or cooking dinner together.

Worship and prayer. Your study will be enhanced by spending time praising God together in prayer or song. Pray for each other's needs—and keep track of how God is answering prayer in your group. Ask God to help you to apply what you are learning in your study.

Outreach. Reaching out to others can be a practical way of applying what you are learning, and it will keep your group from becoming self-focused. Host a series of evangelistic discussions for your friends or neighbors. Clean up the yard of an elderly friend. Serve at a soup kitchen together, or spend a day working in the community.

Many more suggestions and helps in each of these areas are found in the *Small Group Starter Kit*. You will also find information on building a small group. Reading through the starter kit will be worth your time.

Study 1. Loving God Through Worship.
Psalm 116.

Purpose: To understand the nature of a love relationship with God.

Question 1. Look for cause and effect in these verses. Note how the psalmist's experiences have given him an appreciation for God's role in his life.

Question 2. Be sensitive to those in the group who are still seekers or are angry with God. Make it safe for participants to speak freely about their relationship with God, even if they don't love him right now.

Question 3. "The connection in this context [verse 13] to the payment of vows in the temple suggests that a libation is being poured out as testimony is given of God's goodness and protection. Libations were a common form of thanksgiving in the ancient world, as depicted on Egyptian, Phoenician and Mesopotamian reliefs. The libation represents the deliverance (salvation) afforded by deity and also accomplishes deliverance from the vow" (John H. Walton, Victor H. Matthews and Mark W. Chavalas, *The IVP Bible Background Commentary: Old Testament* [Downers Grove, Ill.: InterVarsity Press, 2000], p. 553).

Question 4. Note the contrast between verses 1, 2 and 4, when the psalmist is focusing on God, and verses 3, 10 and 11, where he is focusing on himself. When worship becomes boring, it usually indicates that something is missing in our communication with God.

Question 5. The psalmist first describes supplication—asking God for help—in verses 1-4, then moves on to confession (vv. 8-11), praise and thanksgiving (vv. 12-19). A handy acronym for a balanced prayer life is ACTS—adoration (praise), confession, thanksgiving and supplication.

Question 6. For further reading about the relationship between faith and health see Harold Koenig, M.D., *The Healing Power of Faith: Science Explores Medicine's Last Frontier* (New York: Simon & Schuster, 1999), or Reginald Cherry, M.D., *Healing Prayer: God's Divine Intervention in Medicine, Faith and Prayer* (Nashville: Thomas Nelson, 1999).

Question 7. The psalmist moves from personal conversation with the Lord to formal liturgical worship in the "presence of all his people." According to the *IVP Bible Background Commentary: Old Testament,* "Vows are voluntary, conditional agreements that were common in most of the cultures of the ancient Near East. . . . In the ancient world the most common context for a vow was when a request was being made to deity. The condition would typically involve God's provision or protection, while that which was vowed was usually a gift to deity. The gift would most frequently take the form of a sacrifice, but other types of gifts to the sanctuary or priests would be options. Fulfillment of a vow could usually be accomplished at the sanctuary and was a public act" (pp. 553-54).

Question 9. If the response becomes a gripe session about the worship services group members attend, try to turn the focus on how we can change the way we respond to God in worship. Even a "boring" church service becomes exciting if you are in the presence of the One you love.

Now or Later. According to ancient Hebrew thinking, these terms do not refer to specific organs or parts or the person, but to the whole person in relationship. The term "heart" (Hebrew *leb*) refers to the seat of the emotions, will and reason. The "soul" (Hebrew *nephesh*) describes the person in need, desire and relationship. "Strength" (Hebrew *me'od*) simply means diligently, exceedingly and wholly.

Study 2. Loving God by Serving Others. John 21:1-19.

Purpose: To recognize that our love for God is demonstrated in the way we serve others.

Question 1. Ask the group to consider Peter's uneven history as a disciple. How would going fishing have comforted him in a time like this?

Question 2. John 18:15-18, 25-27 describes how Peter denied Jesus three times before the crucifixion.

Question 4. "The threefold challenge to Peter looks as if it were designed to parallel his threefold denial (15-19). There are differences in the wording of the three questions. In the third question the verb used for *love* (*phileō*) is the same as that used in all Peter's answers, but it differs from the word used in the first two questions (*agapaō*). However, in the NT these two verbs are often used interchangeably, and it seems, therefore, that no special significance can be attached to the different words used. There are also differences in the three charges to Peter. The first and third use the word *feed*, whereas the second uses the word for tend (*take care*), which involves all the responsibilities of shepherding the sheep. The first is directed towards the *lambs*, whereas the second and third are directed towards the *sheep*. These differences carry no theological significance. Peter's third response (17) was stronger than the first two, no doubt called out by his grief in being asked three times.

"The fact that Peter was clearly forgiven by Jesus and given new responsibilities, amounting to apostleship, despite his total denial of his Lord, can give genuine hope to Christians today who feel that they have denied Jesus and that this is unforgivable. He calls only for our repentance and our love" (D. A. Carson et al., eds., New Bible Commentary [Leicester: IVP, 1994], p. 1065).

Question 6. Throughout Scripture the imagery of sheep represents God's people, with God as shepherd (for example, Ps 23; 1 Pet 2:25). Human leaders are also referred to as shepherds who tend the sheep (for example, Is 56:11; Jer 3:15; Ezek 34; Zech 11:4-17; Acts 20:28).

Question 8. "The prediction of v 18 was claimed in tradition to have been fulfilled by Peter being crucified upside down. But the tradition itself is not strongly attested and may be an inference from this passage. In saying Peter would glorify God in his death, John sees him as following the example of Jesus (19). Some think that Peter followed Jesus along the shore, but the 'following' implies something more radical than this, nothing short of commitment to his service. Peter's concern for John and the answer of Jesus, virtually telling him to mind his own business, seems to be related to correct a misunderstanding which was circulating at the time of the publication of the gospel. If John, after a long life, was still alive when the gospel was written (on the assumption of his being the author), it was necessary for the rumour that he was not going to die (23) to be rectified" (D. A. Carson et al., eds., New Bible Commentary, p. 1065).

Question 10. Challenge the group to think of specific ways they can be serving others right now. For example, if some list future goals such as becoming a missionary, a health care professional or a pastor, explore ways that they could minister to others in the name of Christ on campus, in their communities or through short-term missions.

Study 3. Loving God's Word: Our Guide for Life. Psalm 119:97-112.

Purpose: To discover how loving God's Word leads to an ethical life that glorifies God.

Question 1. Encourage the group to look carefully throughout the passage. You might want to list the responses on a large sheet of paper.

Question 2. Again, look throughout the passage and list what the group discovers.

Question 3. Obviously, the Bible is not a physics text or a medical manual; however, it instructs us about God, gives general principles for ethics, morality and interpersonal relationships, as well as an understanding of basic concepts like the nature of human beings and creation, or the meaning and purpose of life, death, health. Examples of ideas that are incompatible with a biblical worldview would include euthanasia, promoting a homosexual lifestyle, advocating worship of "the goddess within" or requiring students to participate in energy-based therapies.

Question 4. As the group discusses these strategies, help them to consider how to be kind and respectful when confronting the instructor, as well as how to build a strong case for a biblical point of view.

Question 5. Set the scene. Ask the group to close their eyes and imagine being in an unfamiliar setting in the dark—the woods, a large building or in a strange city. What obstacles might they encounter? What dangers could be present? How would a light make a difference?

Question 6. Try to encourage thoughtful answers. If most of the suggestions seem superficial, pose some more complex situations where the Bible could shed light but also create some tensions. For example, what insights would the Bible give you if an unmarried friend came to you and tearfully confided that she was pregnant?

Questions 7-8. In a culture that values tolerance and withholding judgment, we hesitate to admit that we have enemies. Help to create a safe atmosphere for participants to talk about troubled relationships in which they feel someone is out to get them. For example, an enemy could be a professor who grades unfairly, an abusive former boyfriend, a colleague who spreads lies, a hostile opponent in a political race, or someone who attacks your faith.

Question 9. Keep prodding until a variety of Bible study approaches are described. For example, personal study could include reading the whole Bible in a year, meditating on short passages, reading a book at a time, using study guides on relevant topics, commentaries, Bible dictionaries and concordances, journaling and Scripture memory. Group study might include one-to-one, small group, sermons and lectures, taking courses, or participating in an online Bible discussion. Discuss the value of each method, considering advantages and drawbacks, as well as how a combination of personal and group study enhances our understanding of Scripture.

Question 10. A heritage is something passed down from previous generations. Challenge participants to consider not only the wealth of saints described in the Bible but also historical figures who made bold stands based on their faithfulness to the Scriptures, as well as family and/or older friends who passed on a legacy of faith through sharing their insights from Scripture.

Study 4. Loving God's Word: Our Standard for Truth.
2 Timothy 3.
Purpose: To consider how we can use the Bible as a guide for everyday life.
Question 1. The first response may be "It's the same!" Encourage the group to describe some specific examples of

these behaviors and discuss what they find offensive about them.

Question 2. These could range from New Age spiritualities to the "health and wealth gospel" (believing that true Christians will be materially blessed and physically healthy). Other examples could include seeking sex, power, status, money, academic success, pleasure or substance abuse.

Question 3. The incidents Paul refers to in Antioch, Iconium and Lystra are described in Acts 13—14. There he experienced both highs and lows, enthusiastic acceptance and persecution. The question is intended to stimulate discussion about the realities of the Christian life, including the hard times we might be called to face.

Questions 4-5. Some in the group may have come to faith as adults, others may have grown up in Christian homes. Even lifelong Christians will have crisis points at which their relationship with God strengthens and matures. Encourage discussion about how the presence of more mature Christians and the Scriptures influenced their Christian growth.

Question 6. For further elaboration, see 2 Peter 1:20-21. Some may bring up questions about inerrancy at this point. You can point out that the Bible was not dictated by God word-for-word as Muslims claim for the Koran, but the Bible represents the lived experience of a very human people who walked with God and heard his voice. It is not intended to be a scientific textbook but to communicate the truth about God, human nature, our environment and the meaning and purpose of life, as well as what lies beyond this life.

Questions 7-8. Discuss various ways we receive biblical teaching—through sermons, lectures, commentaries and other reference books, personal and small group Bible studies—and consider the advantages and disadvantages of each method.

**Study 5. Loving God's People in Their Ethnic Diversity.
Numbers 12.**

Purpose: To recognize that God expects us to love and respect people of all races and ethnic backgrounds.

Group discussion. If the group insists it is open but the membership is homogenous, discuss what may be keeping others away.

Questions 1-3. Help the group to put themselves in the place of Miriam and Aaron. Moses' choice for a wife may have been niggling at them anyhow, but having everyone else complaining about his leadership probably gave them the confidence to challenge him. They may have felt his "poor" choices were reflecting on them. They may have felt jealous that their younger brother was appointed leader over them. Or perhaps they just thought they could do a better job. However, his Cushite wife became the target of their frustrations.

Question 4. Responses might include misperceptions, fear of the unknown, economic concerns (loss of property value, competition for available jobs) and enculturation.

Question 5. Humility is a Christian virtue that is not generally appreciated in our culture either! Ask the group to think of examples of leaders who have demonstrated humility. How did that affect their ability to lead and their esteem in the eyes of the world?

Question 7. The "leprosy" that Miriam experienced was probably some sort of contagious skin disease, not Hansen's disease (what we know as leprosy today). Modern public health still uses isolation as a way of containing communicable diseases. A friend who returned from China with a suspected case of SARS (Severe Acute Respiratory Syndrome) described her enforced isolation in the hospital as more difficult than the disease itself. It became a time of intense introspection and spiritual reflection.

Questions 9-10. Most Christians are not intentionally preju-
diced or unkind, but we become comfortable in our routines
and often forget to include newcomers, or feel reluctant to
change—often without realizing it. How often have you said,
"Everybody knows the words to this song," without thinking of
those who may not? Similarly, we may assume that people of
another racial or ethnic identity may not be interested in our
fellowship group, so we do not make the effort to invite them.

Study 6. Loving God's People into the Kingdom. John 4:4-42.
Purpose: To learn how to engage people in a discussion about
spiritual concerns.
Question 1. This woman literally had three strikes against her.
She was a Samaritan, a woman and probably a prostitute.
   "That this Samaritan woman comes to the well alone rather
than in the company of other women probably indicates that
the rest of the women of Sychar did not like her, in this case
because of her sexual activities. . . . Although Jewish teachers
warned against talking much with women in general, they
would have especially avoided Samaritan women, who, they
declared, were unclean from birth" (Craig S. Keener, *The IVP
Bible Background Commentary: New Testament* [Downers Grove,
Ill.: InterVarsity Press, 1993], p. 272).
Question 2. "Other ancient accounts show that even asking
water of a woman could be interpreted as flirting with her—especially if she had come alone due to a reputation for looseness.
Jesus breaks all the rules of Jewish piety here. In addition, both
Isaac (Gen 24:17) and Jacob (Gen 29:10) met their wives at wells;
such precedent created the sort of potential ambiguity at this well
that religious people wished to avoid altogether" (Keener, *IVP
Bible Background Commentary: New Testament*, p. 272).
Question 3. Encourage the group to look at the whole passage
and note the changing dynamics.

Question 4. See verses 14-15.

Question 5. This woman obviously had some theological background and strong convictions. Although clothed initially in skepticism, she seems to have been a sincere seeker.

Question 6. Notice how Jesus' replies to this woman constantly keep her on her toes. He teases, intrigues, offers her something, but also confronts her with the truth about herself and about God. Keener states, "In view of the ambiguity of the situation . . . her statement, 'I have no husband,' could mean 'I am available.' Jesus removes the ambiguity, which stems from his refusal to observe customs that reflected ethnic and gender prejudice, not from any actual flirtation on his part" (*IVP Bible Background Commentary: New Testament*, p. 273).

Question 9. To summarize, Jesus used the following approaches: (1) He established rapport by affirming that the woman had something important to offer. (2) He treated her with respect and engaged her in conversation. (3) He used something concrete as a metaphor for a spiritual truth. (4) He offered her something that she was seeking. (5) He forced her to confront her sin without condemning her. (6) He waited for an appropriate time to correct her doctrine. (7) He revealed himself at a point when she was ready to hear the truth.

Study 7. Loving God's Purposes: Trusting God's Plan. Jeremiah 29:1-14.

Purpose: To know and trust God's ultimate purposes for our lives.

Question 1. If the group seems stumped, remind them that conquering armies usually takes the brightest and most powerful members of the nations they conquer, essentially creating a "brain drain" in those areas. Not only can they use the expertise of their captives, but also the defeated country will not have the leadership to wage war anytime soon.

Questions 3-4. The activities listed here suggest a long-term commitment to and involvement in the communities in which they lived. If needed, help the group compare this with some-one who thinks in terms of "just passing through"—for example, living in a campus apartment or working for a temporary agency.

Question 5. Seventy is a symbolic number representing divine judgment. It also represented about three generations—a long time.

Questions 6-7. These questions are designed to help the group consider the differences between human plans and God's pur-poses. Often the former make much more sense to us than the latter.

Question 10. There is also a fine line between participating in God's plans and expecting God to bless our plans. We can get so busy doing things for God that we miss his plans for us. Be sure that this does not turn into a session for planning good works. Instead, encourage the group to discern God's will through prayer and studying Scripture.

Study 8. Loving God's Purposes: A Mission from God. Ephesians 1.

Purpose: To understand and participate in God's greater pur-poses for all humankind.

Question 1. Make a list on a chalkboard or large sheet of paper, then review the list asking about the practical application of each.

Question 2. "It was a common Jewish belief that history was moving through many stages to its climax, when everything would be put under God's rule. Some philosophers argued that the whole universe was permeated by God and would be absorbed back into him. Like Jewish writers who adapted the language of such philosophers, Paul believes that history moves toward a climax of subordination to God, not absorption into him" (Keener, *IVP Bible Background Commentary: New Testament,* p. 542).

These may seem like abstract concepts at first. Help the group to think in terms of "God sightings" (glimpses of God at work putting lives back together)—for example, restored relationships, unexplained healings, friends becoming Christians or even getting a good grade on the test you expected to fail. This personal involvement of God in our daily lives is radically different from the idea of God as an "energy field" into which human beings will simply be absorbed at death.

Question 3. This is referring to the biblical concept of *shalom.* In other words, it is whatever we do to create a God-centered community that offers salvation, acceptance, peace, health, physical care, nurturing and economic support. Encourage the group to think locally at first, then globally.

Question 4. Try to keep the discussion from getting hung up on predestination versus freewill. The point here is that God personally chose each of us and "desires everyone to be saved and to come to the knowledge of the truth" (1 Tim 2:4 NRSV). We are saved in order to share that salvation with those who do not yet know him.

Question 5. Note that Paul was giving thanks for those who had become Christians through his witness and were now passing on the faith to others.

Question 7. Paul prayed for the early Christians to experience these things to equip them for ministry, not merely to give them a good feeling.

Questions 8-9. In these verses, Paul is emphasizing Christ's victory over all demonic powers. Furthermore, if God's power could raise Jesus from the dead, we can be confident that not only will he give us victory over the power of evil in our life now, he will also eventually raise us from the dead.

Question 10. The church is a very human organization, but at the same time, it is the visible body of Christ. Help the group to think of specific ways that their congregation is ministering to people in their community and beyond.

Prayer. You may want to break off into pairs and pray these verses for each other.

Judith Allen Shelly was publications director of Nurses Christian Fellowship, director of NCF Press and editor of the Journal of Christian Nursing. *She has written many books and articles and her editorial work has won numerous awards.*